The Happy Herd

Bryce Walton

Alpha Editions

This edition published in 2022

ISBN : 9789356230903

Design and Setting By
Alpha Editions
www.alphaedis.com
Email - info@alphaedis.com

As per information held with us this book is in Public Domain.
This book is a reproduction of an important historical work. Alpha Editions uses the best technology to reproduce historical work in the same manner it was first published to preserve its original nature. Any marks or number seen are left intentionally to preserve its true form.

THE HAPPY HERD

BY BRYCE WALTON

The Captain told Kane to take his cushion pills, that they were contacting the pits at La Guardia within half an hour.

"I still can't figure you," the Captain said. "Up there, just you and your wife for sixteen years. That's a hell of a long time."

Kane smiled. He had been almost completely out of touch with the world for sixteen years, and it surprised him a little that anyone thought it remarkable in any way. Particularly the Captain who spent most of his time, too, alone.

But the Captain was genuinely perturbed about it. The authorities had abandoned the space-station project. Abandoned the Martian project. They had taken away the other three ships from the Moon-run, and there was no explanation for it at all.

The rest of the Captain's crew, except an old atomics man, had drifted away and never come back, and the Captain had been unable to find out anything whatsoever about what had happened to them. He had never heard from them again. They had never been replaced.

But the Captain couldn't seem to define what it was he was warning Kane to be wary of down there.

"I haven't left my ship for years, Professor Kane, and that's the truth. I take on supplies and see to the ore getting into the holds but when those machines up there that do the digging and loading wear out, they won't be replaced. Just no interest in space any more. I can tell.

"I stay on the ship, with my wife, see. And the few guys down there around the field at La Guardia I have to rub up against—why, sir, they treat me as if I had some kind of contagious disease!

"But they need this ore I'm bringing back here now, so they leave me alone."

"Who leaves you alone?"

"Whoever didn't leave the rest of my crew alone. Whoever sang 'em the old siren song, that's who. Once a spaceman, always a spaceman, sir. And not a one of those men pulled out because he wanted to do it! That's what I'm saying. And I'm telling you to watch out. I'm blasting off for the Moon again on the 25th. I hope you're aboard."

Kane shrugged as the Captain bowed out, making disgruntled noises in his throat. He was getting along in years, Kane reasoned, and was probably just expressing that fact, externalizing some way or another. Still, what he had said was odd—

The truth was, Kane had been inexcusably out of contact with the world.

The pills dulled his senses and he began to fall asleep on the pneumatic couch. He thought of the years of work on his theories concerning the unified fields in the formulation of spatial matter. He thought of Helen, the good years together before her sudden death, sharing love and work, how complete and full and good it had been. During all those sixteen years he couldn't recall a moment of real boredom.

He hadn't missed life on Earth. When a man has one full love and his work, he's isolated no matter where he is, even in the middle of New York City.

He had ten notebooks full of notes in his briefcase. It would open their eyes, a really basic new theory that would defy the pessimistic theory of entropy, and its assurance of an inevitable death of all things.

Finding another wife to replace Helen wouldn't be easy of course. A new relationship would be different, but it should be as good. It might require some difficulties which he had anticipated and was prepared for. He was only forty-six. He had a long time to look. He was in excellent physical condition and was not unattractive, though of course that wasn't the real issue either way.

He wanted love, a companion, someone who could truly share in his work. Who would love that observatory in Albetagnius crater as a home for the rest of her life.

He woke up, and prepared to leave the ship. He carried his briefcase with his notes in it. The rest of his luggage would follow later. According to Phil Nordson, there was a suite reserved for him at the Midtown Hotel at 50th and Madison Avenue.

He climbed down the ladder to the exit. The door was open and a heavy fog drifted past the opening, but a small dark car with two drivers waited outside.

As Kane stepped down the gangplank, one of the figures, a woman in a light blue uniform, jumped out and opened the door for him.

Interest and excitement rose in Kane as the car moved through the mist toward the terminal where he was to meet Phil. It would probably do him good, get away from his work, different surroundings, just rest up a little. Even live it up a little perhaps. There would be parties, and he wanted to see a little of the country. Maybe visit some of Helen's relatives in the Middle West, and he certainly wanted to have some long bull sessions with Professors Martinson and Legmann over at the University.

Then there was the question of meeting the right kind of woman. That was something only the fates could decide, Kane thought. He was no romantic, but that sort of thing wasn't something you could figure out in advance, plot out like an equation. It wasn't anything you could handle with personality charts, though they had been trying that when he'd left. The personality you could measure with gadgets was such a small part of it really....

But Phil would arrange for the social activities. As he recalled his old schoolmate, he remembered that Phil was a very social kind of fellow. Phil had thought it was absurd, Kane's volunteering for that job in Albetagnius. Phil hadn't even gone on to post-graduate work in electronics, his chosen field. Phil had gone right out to accept a position with Isotopics Unlimited, somewhere in New Jersey.

They had corresponded for a while; and the cablegram from Phil had expressed Phil's delight at Kane's decision to return to Earth.

The car stopped before the well-lighted entrance to terminal building No. 214 and the woman hopped out, opened the door for Kane. He went inside the building, feeling the abnormally heavy pull of gravity. He had grown accustomed to the gravity on the Moon, and though his body was already starting to adapt itself, it would take time, and he was beginning to feel the drag.

Phil was there waiting. He hadn't mentioned anyone else being there, and Kane certainly didn't expect anyone else. He didn't know anyone really, no one other than Phil except Martin and Legmann. But there was Phil, and a number of people around him, and they were all rushing toward Kane, smiling, shouting, waving their arms. Phil looked much the same, tall and flashily dressed, thin and good looking as always, but with hair slightly greying.

The others, men, women, various ages and sizes, waving scarfs and circling eagerly around Kane, broke out in a happy chorus of mixed voices:

Greetings! Welcome, Old Friend Kane!

Welcome home to Earth again.

Kane felt a brief compulsion to retreat, but that was absurd.

"Good to see you, Prof!" Phil shouted.

"Hello, Phil." Someone grabbed his briefcase. Kane tried to get it back but it was gone among the frothing arms and milling bodies.

"We'll take care of it, Kane boy," Phil said. His arm was over Kane's shoulders. Several women were hanging onto Kane's arms. Healthy, tanned, lovely women.

"Sure glad to see you, Prof. Aren't we?"

A chorus enthusiastically shrieked, "Yes!"

Kane felt some embarrassment. He was being crowded out an exit toward a line of cabs. Several shiny ten-foot saucers with railings around them whirred past and disappeared in the fog. All of them had two or more people on them, and from the sound, there were quite a number of them up in the fog somewhere.

"We've all got a saucer now," Phil said. "Only we have to take cabs over to Lucie's house. This way we can all ride together. We can all get into two cabs, can't we, gang?"

"Yes!"

"Lucie?" Kane asked as they crowded around the two cabs. Who were these people? Friends of Phil's of course.

"We're Lucie," the woman said softly. Kane caught a glimpse of a mature face and a lovely figure. The face was odd, Kane thought, the maturity seeming to be disguised by an insincere smile. What a peculiar way of introducing oneself....

"We're having a little party at the house," Lucille said. "Aren't we?"

"Yes!"

"We've got lots of fun planned for us, Kane boy," Phil said.

Kane remembered a look of sardonic mockery in Lucille's eyes as her face disappeared and was replaced by several others.

Somehow, Kane couldn't figure out how, five of them were jammed into the back seat of one of the cabs and then they were moving away through the fog.

Someone who said "We're Laura," with a tight tanned body was wriggling on Kane's lap and her arm was around Kane's neck. She had bright teeth and she breathed scentedly into Kane's face.

"Nothing to worry about, Kane boy," he heard Phil say in a muffled joy. "We're the gang."

"'It's always fair weather, the Sunhill Gang is always together,'" Laura was crooning. The red-faced fat man next to Kane laughed and then Kane saw that the red-faced man whose name seemed to be Ben and the woman on his lap whom he called Jenny, were kissing one another. There was something embarrassingly intimate about the way they did it. It was suddenly much more than a mere spontaneous show of affection.

Kane looked away. Beyond a certain point, he felt that love-making was something that should be reserved for privacy.

That sort of thing might be expected to change, of course. Customs changed, and as Kane recalled, one could say the trend had been somewhat in that direction.

There were two drivers up front. That was a change too. Every cab had had two drivers, a man and a woman.

It was all a bit overdone, Kane thought. Still, they were friends of Phil's. A friend of yours is a friend of mine.

But it affected Kane adversely. He felt uneasy. He didn't really know them at all. In fact, he scarcely even knew Phil.

"We're so glad with you," the girl on Kane's lap said. She crushed her lips over his mouth and pressed her body against him. Kane couldn't say that was affecting him adversely. In fact, if there weren't all these other people around—

"We're nice together," Laura breathed against his lips.

Everyone was so damn glad to see him. All they needed were banners, little pins. Official Welcoming Party to Greet the Arrival of Professor Larry Kane.

Kane managed to look out the window as they crossed the Tri-Borough Bridge at 125th Street and started up the East River Drive.

"Things haven't changed much," Kane said. "Not nearly so much traffic though."

"The saucers," Phil said. "Most of the traffic's up in the air."

"We're looking at things," Laura said.

"Great old town," Ben said and laughed, on and on. Jenny laughed too, then said. "It looks just the same almost as when we left."

They're all speaking for me. Kane thought. Funny, a damned funny custom. It was a reflection of something else. What did it really mean? His feeling of unease seemed exaggerated. But then their efforts to make him welcome seemed pretty exaggerated too....

"Everybody happy?" the fat man yelled.

"Yes!"

"We're happy aren't we, honey," Laura said.

"Sure," Kane said.

Why not?

Kane noticed the amazing dearth of traffic on Madison Avenue.

No traffic cops either. That had changed too. One thing you had always been sure of seeing and that was a cop in New York.

When Kane asked about it, the smiles almost fled from every face, and the moment of silence seemed like a form of shock. Kane realized then that there hadn't been even a second of silence before then.

"It's hard to realize we've been away so long," Phil finally said.

"I'm really tired," Kane said to Phil as they went on past the Midtown Hotel toward Lucille's apartment. "I was intending to go directly to the hotel and rest up a while—"

"We'll relax at Lucie's," Jenny said. "We got music, we got music, we got music, who could ask for anything more?"

"But—" Kane started to protest at least mildly, but the rest of the sentence was blotted out by a long kiss from Laura.

They had all crowded into an elevator, and then rushed into Lucille's apartment on a high level of The Sunny Hill building near Washington Square. The apartment consisted of one huge room with a circular couch in the middle upon which everyone immediately sat.

Laura sat beside Kane who was getting more tired every minute. There was just enough room for the gang to squeeze up tight to one another in a circle around a table supporting some kind of machine with wires that were immediately run from it and attached to everyone's wrist, and to a narrow metal headband with which everyone's head was crowned.

Kane was listening to music. It was like being dropped unexpectedly into the middle of a large symphony orchestra. The sound seemed to pulse and vibrate gigantically all around him. It was more than merely listening. He was in it. He felt himself a part of it, swimming in it, and almost fighting to keep from being carried away by what seemed to be perfectly recorded music that was now being delivered by some final form of hi-fi.

The music itself was familiar enough. Instrumentalized opera arias orchestrated on a fantastic scale. The quantity was so great that sensitivity as to quality was dulled. Kane, shocked by thunderous sweeps of sheer volume gave way before the sound. It wasn't sleep. He could hardly say he rested, but he was in a semi-stupor. When he glanced at his watch sometime later, two hours and some minutes had passed.

The wires were being removed from wrists, headbands from heads. Kane's head ached slightly. Everyone was reaching as cards fell out of the machine in the middle.

Laura handed one to Kane. It was covered with symbols in the form of some kind of graph, but he couldn't decipher it.

There was a great deal of chatter, musical jargon, colloquial in both space and time, most of it eluding comprehension. Kane stood there holding his card as everyone milled around one another.

Phil said, "Let's see how we liked it, Prof?"

That seemed to have been the general idea—how much everyone liked the music. And each one looked at his card, and they were all comparing cards and exclaiming over them.

Phil was looking at Kane's card, comparing it with his own and with some other cards.

"Well, not bad," Phil was saying, "Is it, gang?"

"Not bad at all!" they chorused.

"What isn't bad?" Kane asked.

"Our taste, man," Laura said. "You'll fit so good."

The odd one, Lucille, raised an eyebrow, with some mockery in it still, at Kane.

"You'll sure belong, Professor. Don't worry," Lucille said. She held up her card. "We liked it."

"Of course it'll take a little time," Phil said as he threw his arm over Kane's shoulder. "A few sessions and you'll match up just right."

"I really don't believe I understand," Kane said vaguely.

"You will," Lucille said as she moved away from him. "You sure will, Professor." She was tall, and with long lithe legs. She was a handsome woman, Kane thought.

As Phil explained casually on the way toward the Midtown Hotel, they had just had a music session. Everything was done in sessions, in groups that is. Everyone had his group, and his group did everything together.

Anyway, they had had a music session. The machine in the middle was a Reacto. The cards were Reacto Cards. It was really a kind of taste tester, and the point was that the Reacto tested everyone's reaction to the music.

The cards enabled everyone to check their reactions, check them against the reactions of all the others. It involved conformity ratings, and tendencies to stray from the group norm.

The important thing about the taste rate cards was that they enabled you to find out just how much group spirit you had. The closer your card resembled that of all the others in your group, the more GS you had.

"My GS rating's gone up," Laura kept burbling all the way to the Midtown Hotel. "It's gone up!"

The same process applied to reading, movies, television, eating, anything involving the elements of reacting. The important thing was not how you yourself felt, but how you felt in relation to the feelings of the group. The problem seemed to be that of reducing deviation tendencies to a minimum.

On the way to the Midtown Hotel, Jenny asked Phil how he liked the new best-seller, *Love Is Forever*, and Phil took a small card out of his wallet and they all compared Reacto Cards in order to determine relative reactions to *Love Is Forever*.

Good God! *You had to look at a card to find out how you liked something!* It was frightening as hell.

Kane wondered how wide-spread, how universal, it really was, this incredible conformity, this collective thinking.

This appalling sacrifice of individuality.

Kane was too tired to give much thought to it right then. He was anxious to get to the Hotel, and he was beginning to fantasize a bed, cool sheets, his body stretching and sinking down into blissful slumber.

But as appalling as the situation seemed at the time, Kane soon found that he had only circled on the fringes of it. This was only the beginning.

"Here we are, here were are, gang!" someone shouted as they piled out of the cabs and Kane was being hustled toward the suddenly formidable glint of a revolving door.

So here we are, Kane thought. It was nice being here all right. He was glad, very glad. But it sounded as though someone might swoon over the fact.

There was some difficulty with the revolving door. No one seemed able to move first, and there were spontaneous group lunges ending in jamming chaos in which someone hurt their arm. Kane thought it was the fat man, Ben.

"We're hurt!" Jenny screamed.

"Oh—it's not bad," Ben said, laughing all the time he was groaning. "Just bruised a little, gang. We're just bruised a little."

Kane grabbed his advantage and ventured alone through the revolving doors into the lobby. A pair of desk clerks nodded across the lobby. A group was emerging from behind drapes and beyond them Kane saw an ornate, subtly lighted, cocktail lounge.

Kane was heading for the elevator when the gang overtook him.

Laura had hold of one of his arms, and Phil the other.

"We're having cocktails," Laura said.

Phil repeated it, and Ben and Jenny joined in. The young man, Clarence, was singing as he herded the others toward the drapes of the cocktail lounge, and they were all whisking Kane away before he could voice any protest.

"What'll the gang have?" the waiter asked, smiling. Only he wasn't really smiling at any of them, Kane thought. He had picked out a center point of focus and was smiling at that so as not to appear to be smiling at any one, but at everyone.

"Martinis!" several voices said.

The waiter nodded, whirled away.

"Ah, waiter," Kane said. "I'll have a double shot of Scotch. No ice."

The waiter seemed shocked, unable to come to grips with Kane's seemingly simple order. "But—but I thought you said Martini."

The gang was still smiling, but faintly. The waiter was backing away.

"No," Kane insisted. "He said Martinis, and she said Martinis, and so did several others. But I didn't say Martinis. I said Scotch, no ice."

"But Martinis—"

Ben forced a pained laugh. "But we ordered Martinis."

"Martinis," Laura said.

"The ayes always have it," Kane heard Lucille whisper near him.

Phil said, with a kind of shaky joviality. "Martinis—"

"Gin makes me ill," Kane said. "For me, it has to be Scotch."

Phil whispered. "Scotch."

"Scotch," the waiter said.

A jukebox in a far corner blasted out from a sea of bubbling, multicolored light.

We're all pals togetherrrrrrr.

The Gang knows no bad weatherrrrrr.

We're all for us all for us,

And we're rolling do-own life's highway,

On our crowded bussssss!

Laura whispered huskily in his ear. "Don't worry about any little old thing. We're one together, man."

God, he was tired. He was so tired he could hardly sit there. He felt numb, and there was desperation under the numbness. Kane wanted to get off somewhere by himself so he could rest, sleep, and think. He wanted to think....

Bits of information drifted haphazardly into Kane's consciousness from the conversation. He had ordered another double Scotch and was almost through with it. He was passing out, but held to conscious awareness by the unceasing banter, laughter and the jukebox—like a marionette held up with wires.

If he suddenly found himself alone in silence, he knew he would collapse instantly.

It seemed that this was a group with a certain common Reacto level, and they all worked in the same place, and lived in the same section of a big housing project, a place called Sunny Hill.

Phil was their Integrator, and he was also an Official in the Isotopic Corporation where the Group worked. Phil was an Integrator for the Isotopic Corporation, a sort of personnel man whose main duty was the integration of the employees' private lives.

When Kane tried to find out about the work itself, no one seemed interested enough to respond. The work was relatively unimportant. The emphasis seemed to be centered almost completely on how people got along together. If your Reacto cards reported a general reaction that strayed too far from your Group norm, you were either sent to another group, or sent to a Staff.

A Staff was a rather vague term for specialists in Integration on a clinical level.

The job was always referred to as "our job", and the Gang seemed to do practically everything together.

Someone mentioned that a friend hadn't been competent in group relations at school and had been Processed. Kane didn't like the words they were so casually throwing around. In fact Kane didn't like any of it, and he was liking it less all the time.

Another term that referred to some sort of adjustment process was the word homogenized. Someone had been "homogenized".

Once Kane tried to find out about his old friends, Professors Legmann, and Martin over at New York University. Phil avoided the question for a time, then finally admitted that Martin was still there in the archeology department, but that Legmann had quit the profession years ago. "He quit teaching and became a plumber."

"A plumber?" Kane whispered. "Legmann?"

"That's right," Phil grinned.

"We're all plumbing together," Laura lisped.

"But—that's preposterous!" Kane almost yelled. "Legmann—why he was the finest research chemist—"

"But he wasn't really happy in his profession," Phil said. "As I recall—he just wasn't well adjusted as a research chemist and teacher."

"Who said he wasn't?"

"Why the Staff."

"What Staff—?"

"Anyway, he's a plumber now somewhere," Phil said. "He's happy now."

Kane felt a coldness on his neck. His stomach seemed to turn completely over. The devil with this, he thought. His eyeballs felt as though they were covered with sand, and his lids seemed leaded weights. He pushed back his chair.

"You'll excuse me," he said. "But I'm really tired out. I'm going to get some rest—"

"But the night's young for us, man," Laura shrieked.

"We're having more Scotch," Lucille said, watching him carefully.

"Fun time's only starting for us," the young man protested, and the fat man and Jenny and all of them protested loudly together, laughing all the while.

Kane was backing away. The hell with them. He turned and ran for the elevator. Then he remembered that he didn't know what room he was supposed to be checked into. He didn't have a key either. He—

Two smiling men, were on either side of him. In a mirror he could see the half smiling, half concerned faces of Phil and Laura, and the slightly sardonic eyes of Lucille.

"Don't worry, Gang," he heard Phil say. "We're taking a Special room. We'll be together again soon."

"This way," the two young smiling men said. They wore uniforms and appeared to be bellhops. "We'll show you to our room."

The two bellhops started to back out of the room. "What's special about it?" Kane asked. "Only thing I can see about it that could be considered special is that it's about big enough to be someone's closet! I reserved a suite. What kind of a run-around is this anyway?"

It was hardly bigger than a large closet. A white room, with only a single bed in it, and a bureau. Through a narrow, partly open door, he could see a bathroom, and that was it.

"Well," the bellhop said, smiling. "It's our Single."

"You mean you call it special because it's a single," Kane asked.

The bellhops nodded.

"Why?" Kane insisted. "What's special about a single?"

"We only have one single here," the bellhops said. "We hope you are comfortable with us, Professor Kane."

"Look here! Why should you only have one single in this entire hotel? And what's so special about it?"

"This single is seldom demanded by guests," the bellhop said.

"I didn't demand it. I reserved a suite, or at least I understood that my friend, Phil Nordson, reserved a suite. I certainly didn't demand this!"

"But—but of course you did. We have to have a single when we're—not getting along well with ourselves."

Kane started for the door, but the two men backed out and shut it in his face. He tried the knob. The door was locked. He turned quickly and scanned the room, but there was no key visible. Then one of the curtains moved as he walked toward it, and he saw that the narrow window was barred.

As he swept the curtains aside to look out through the bars, and grabbed at the bars in a kind of instinctual gesture, a metal panel slid noiselessly across and shut out a flash of neon light.

He was alone, locked up like a dangerous madman!

By the head of the narrow bed that resembled something antiseptic in a barracks, Kane saw the black eye of a phone peeking out of a niche in the wall.

He pulled it out and jabbed at a button. His throat felt tight and he could feel the pounding of his heart as he leaned against the wall.

"This is Professor Kane, room 2004."

"Yes, we're here."

"And I'm here! In this ridiculous closet. I'm locked in. There must be some sort of mistake. The window—"

"We'll be all right. We'll be fine in a little while."

"Look here—connect me with the cocktail lounge. I want to speak with Phil Nordson. Yes, he's there—"

He heard nothing, absolutely nothing, except his own heart. No clock in the room either. The walls and ceiling had a peculiar grained look.

"Hello, Prof!"

"Phil! Phil, listen, what in the name of God goes on here? I'm locked in! You said you reserved a suite for me, and this room—"

"We aren't going to worry," Phil said. Kane heard laughter in the background and the high-pitched choral voices from the jukebox. "We'll be all right. We figured there would be a little trouble here and there, at first."

"I don't give a damn about a little trouble there! Phil, I'm talking about me, here! I'm locked in. And my luggage. Where is it? And—"

Kane's stomach jumped. A kind of terror hit him like a cold breath. "Phil! My briefcase. Where's my briefcase?"

"We have it somewhere—" Phil was saying. "Just don't let us worry."

Kane heard a clicking sound somewhere and he yelled into the phone but nothing came back. He released the phone and it was sucked back into the wall.

He sank down on the bed and fumbled absently at his coat and then at his necktie. The walls had a blurred quality and he felt on the edge of passing out. He kept thinking of the briefcase, with years of work in it, the equations, more than could be preserved entirely in a man's head.

It was too sickening to think about, the possibility of them losing his briefcase. Phil didn't seem concerned. No one was concerned with his briefcase, that was obvious. The only thing they were concerned about was that he didn't get along with the Gang.

The hell with the Gang, every last one of the Gang. If he never heard of the Gang or saw the Gang again, he would consider himself extremely fortunate.

He felt numb, too tired to think about anything. He fumbled at one shoe, got it off, then worked vaguely at the other one. He would rest, sleep, sleep for a long time, then he would be able to think. He might find this all exaggerated, unreal, once he slept, rested, woke up again.

A man certainly had rights. There was some authority he could contact of course. He was just too upset to think about it anymore.

He had his shirt, his undershirt off. He had his shoes and socks off and he flexed his feet in ecstasy. He unzipped his fly and as he started to stand up to take his pants off, he groaned with fright and fell backward onto the bed.

A chair fused with the bed. Laura was there, sitting on the chair, but also practically sitting in Kane's lap.

He blinked rapidly and reached out, and his hand moved through the image of Laura, only Laura seemed solid, three-dimensional, very real indeed. Too real.

"Get out," he whispered. "What—"

Glass clinked loudly right in the room with him. The jukebox blared.

Kane couldn't move. He sat rigidly, and the table was there, and all the Gang around it, and Phil there smiling and they were all around Kane drinking Scotch, double shots of Scotch, no ice.

Lucille looked across the table and shook her lovely head slightly. There was concern, genuine concern, a kind of sadness, behind the false smile. The smile, he knew, was for the others. But the concern was for him.

Phil raised his glass. Nine glasses were in the air.

"Here's to us, happy Gang, Prof," Phil shouted.

"Here's to us! Here's to Sunny Hill!" they shouted.

Kane slowly moistened his lips. The three walls and the ceiling had come alive. They were actually huge TV screens, and the effect was startlingly three-dimensional. Only the absence of touch could break the illusion. But the visual and the audial made up for the absence of touch. Kane didn't want to touch them anyway. He wanted them to go away, altogether.

His room was crammed with phantoms from the cocktail lounge. In fact, his room was fused with the cocktail lounge. It was all there somehow.

"Go to sleepy-bye," Laura whispered and made a very suggestive gesture. Her cheeks were flushed as she leaned into and through him.

"Take ourselves a good long snooze," Phil grinned. "Don't worry. The Gang's all here."

Lucille said, hardly smiling at all. "No, don't worry, Professor. We'll all sleep with you."

He zipped his pants back up and slid back through several phantom shapes and pressed against the wall.

"Phil," he finally said. "Phil!"

"Aren't you sleepy now?" Phil asked.

"He's sleepy," Laura said. "We're sleeping with you, Professor man."

"Yes, yes I am sleepy. Goodnight now," Kane said. "Goodnight."

He waited. They didn't take the hint. To them it was no hint at all. He knew they weren't going away. He knew that no matter what he said or did, they wouldn't go away. That was the thing he understood, incredible as it was, he knew now that no matter what he said or did, they wouldn't go away.

They only understood that he was somehow ill. He knew that too. They were right, so he was wrong. They thought they were doing what was best for him. That was obvious. It was all over their faces and actions. If they had any idea how he felt, they still considered his feelings only symptoms of some kind, and they seemed confident that Kane would soon be all right.

But his being all right had nothing to do with their going away.

Kane decided not to give way, not to scream or anything absurd like that. It wouldn't do any good. Calm, be calm and—well maybe just try pretending they're not there at all.

Then he remembered the bathroom and ran through several chairs, a table, and three people, and into the bathroom. He slammed the door and leaned against it and let out a long relieved breath.

He was taking off his shorts when the bathroom walls and the ceiling came alive.

What had been labeled "Boy's Room" down in the cocktail lounge was being projected into the bathroom of room 2004.

It wasn't false modesty that prompted Kane's moan. It wasn't any form of prudishness that moved Kane to clutch his undershorts to his body and leap into the shower stall.

It was a panicky realization of the absolutely involuntary nature of the way things were. Strangers, with friendly smiles, everywhere around him all the time, and he, Larry Kane, had nothing—*absolutely nothing to say about it.*

The shower stall with the pulled curtain was no refuge either. There was a superimposed sink in there on the wall with a phantom shape using an electric razor.

Phil and Ben were leaning through the shower curtain. They weren't there for anything specific. They were just there, chatting, smiling, bantering.

Others came in and out of the "Boy's Room" of the cocktail lounge. Everyone said hello, or directed some sort of friendly comment casually at Kane as though superimposed washrooms were the quintessence of social normalcy. And, Kane thought pushing hard at panic, they probably were.

Phil and Ben were there for no other reason than to keep Kane company. To help him. He could see that. No matter how tortured he seemed, their attitude remained that of beneficence. The trouble was all his, and they gave no indication of seeing his side of anything.

Evidently, to them, being alone was the worst thing that could happen to anybody. If he wanted to be alone then he was wrong, he was sick, he was put in a special room. A single. But they wouldn't go away.

He managed to turn on the shower, and he turned his face up to the icy water and closed his eyes and imagined he was back in blessed isolation in the study of the observatory on the Moon. But it was a long long way back to the Moon.

It worked both ways. He could see and hear them. They could hear and see him too, but he determined to do his best to ignore them. The idea of social amenities no longer bothered Kane. Being impolite was an absurdity. Social decency was a mutual thing, and these people weren't considering his rights at all.

He finished his shower and draped the towel around his waist and went back out into the closet they had given him. He walked toward the bed, sidestepping people, chairs, tables still unable to realize fully that these things weren't really here.

The jukebox got louder. A couple danced through him. Suddenly, Kane stood shivering, a raw panic taking hold. Control fled before the rising jukebox clangor, the laughter, the waving and shouting and hideous unwelcome demons of camaraderie.

He felt himself wildly waving his arms about and shouting at the walls.

"Get out! For God's sake get out and let me sleep!"

Ben was staring at Kane from only a few inches away.

"You," Kane pointed a finger at the three dimensional ghost. "You—fade out, go away somewhere. No—no, Phil, not you. Get these other people out. I want to talk to you—Phil—"

"Easy now," Phil said soothingly. "We'll be all right. In a little while now—"

"I am all right, but I won't be if I can't sleep. Phil—can't all this just—just be tuned out or something?"

Kane tried to imagine none of the others were there. Just the small room, himself, and Phil. But the others were all looking at Kane, all of them looking, all of them smiling. Lucille was looking too, but somehow he was sure he could see a reflection of his own feelings in her eyes, hidden, but there.

"We'll be with you all the way," Phil said.

"But how can I sleep with a cocktail lounge full of people all over my bed? Tell me. I'm listening. Tell me how!"

Phil's smile disappeared completely for a brief second. He whispered, close to Kane's ear. "Try to do it, Larry. Please—*try*!"

Kane ran to the wall, clicked the light switch. He knew that the lights in his room went out, but the slightly dimmer lights projected from the cocktail lounge remained. Somehow, that was even worse. It seemed to resemble the implacable characters of a persisting nightmare. Subdued, with the coruscating bubbling play of multicolored light from the jukebox turning a rainbow over and over the ceiling and the bed, and the Gang, the Gang all there like ghosts with greenish faces smiling, sitting, whispering round the bed.

Kane threw himself on the bed and covered his eyes with his arms.

He was going mad with fatigue, and yet he knew he could never sleep, never rest, under these circumstances. It wasn't just the figures there, the lights, the laughter and whispering and the chorus breaking from the jukebox. It was what their being there really meant, the suggestion of the bigger cause behind what was happening to Kane.

A man who fears to sleep in the dark is not really afraid of the dark. But of what is hiding in it.

Shadows moved above his closed lids. Glass tinkled with ice cubes. Under his sweating forearm, his eyes throbbed and his body felt as though the skin had been scraped all over until it was raw.

Kane propped himself on an elbow, and looked to one side at Phil. Phil grinned sympathetically. Laura was in the same cushioned chair, but she seemed to be sitting beside Kane on the bed. Lucille was avoiding looking at Kane.

"Phil."

"Well, Prof, we thought we were getting our sleep!"

"No," Kane whispered. "I can't sleep. I'm asking you, you Phil, and all the rest of you, to let me sleep. I'm asking you to help me in that way, just for a while. I'm imploring you really to just tune yourselves out for a while and let me sleep."

There was something blank, uncomprehending in the way they smiled at him. Kane knew then that they could never allow themselves to try to understand his situation, because then they might question their own. For example, if they've taken refuge in one another from a terrible fear of insecurity, anxiety, and aloneness, then Kane could only represent the threat of reawakened fear.

What was the use?

"We'll turn the lights down low, how would that be, Prof?" Phil asked.

"We'd like that," Laura whispered.

"Don't be afraid, we're with you," Ben said.

"We'll sing you into dreamland," Jenny said.

"Don't be afraid. We're all together and our Gang is with you," someone else said. It didn't matter who really, Kane thought, because they all spoke not as individuals but as the Gang.

"Through sunshine and in shadow," Lucille said.

The lights dimmed slowly as Kane curled up on the bed and clenched his eyes shut. He pulled the sheet up over his face. He pressed his fingers into his ears. But it wouldn't work. Nothing like that would do any good. You couldn't shut off indignity such as this. You couldn't block out such an intrusion of spirit and human dignity by burying your head, or pressing your ears.

You could try, but not very long, not when you knew it wouldn't do any good.

He had no idea now what time it was, how long he had been here. He had tried to spot a wall clock somewhere in the cocktail lounge, but none was within view. That didn't help either, this timeless feeling. That only enhanced the similarity it all had to a persisting nightmare.

It was a gnawing murmur all around him. It was like a hollow tooth. The softened sounds of their voices going on and on was maddening because they were softened. Softened for him, yet they were still there. He felt like an irritated baby sleeping while adults talked, pretending to soften their voices.

His body was slimy with sweat, and his head pounded with a dull ache. He jumped out of bed and ran straight through Laura to the wall and jerked the phone from its slot.

He yelled into it.

"This is Professor Larry Kane. Room 2004. I'm checking out. Send someone up here with a key! I said send someone up here...."

"We understand, Professor Kane."

"Then you'll send someone up immediately with a key!"

"Please don't get upset. The Staff has been busy, but now the Staff will soon be with you."

The Staff....

"I just want a key, I want to get the hell out of here!"

Kane yelled several times into the phone after the click, but no voice came back. He had grabbed up the table, the metal table at the head of the bed, and flung it into the wall before he realized what he was doing.

The shadows moved toward him. Phil, Laura, Ben, Jenny, Lawrence, Lucille, all the others, nameless, what did it matter anyway, their names?

They were smiling, holding out their arms to him. Compassionate, sympathy, they had it all. All they wanted to do was help him.

He ran through them back toward the bathroom. It was still full of men from the downstairs john. "What time is it?" Kane yelled at someone with a paper towel pressed to his eyes.

"'Bout three I'd say, what a night!"

"Three—"

Three o'clock in the morning, but the fact was Kane wasn't sure about the day. He backed out of the bathroom, slammed the door.

"The Staff is ready, Prof," Phil said.

"We're all with you, aren't we?" Laura giggled.

The closet.

Kane ran into the closet and slammed the door. There was something immediately cozy in the narrow black confines of the closet. Either closet walls weren't TV screens, or they had decided to let him sleep at last. Probably the former. Better convert closets to Television. In case kiddies misbehave and get locked in the closet, they'll not be alone in there....

He curled up on the floor in the pitch blackness and almost immediately began to drift off into sleep. The narrow darkness tightened around him like a thick comforting blanket on a cold night....

Sometime later—he had no idea how much time had passed—a light was blinking at his lids. He opened them slowly and stared into a flickering yellow eye.

A doorhinge creaked. Up there somewhere a voice said pleasantly:

"Professor Kane, your Staff is here."

"Staff?" he whispered, trying to see above the blinking light.

"We're here."

The TV walls were dead now, but that was hardly consoling. The overhead light was glaring with an intense whiteness. The three members of the Staff were busy, and Kane was being Tested.

Kane had emerged from the closet determined to remain as rational as possible, to control his emotions, and find out what he could about his human rights as an individual.

That was easy to find out and only required a few questions honestly and frankly answered.

As a minority, Kane had no rights whatsoever.

He had one big right, the right to think as the majority did. But that didn't count for much yet because Kane was ill, maladjusted and had anti-group feeling.

The Staff was going to test him, find out what was wrong with Kane. And this of course implied that when they found out what was wrong, the difficulty would be taken care of.

The Staff was kind, considerate, almost excessively polite considering the circumstances. They were young efficient men with crewcuts, briefcases, and wearing tight conservative dark suits. Only slight differences in build distinguished them one from another, but this superficial outward difference only seemed to emphasize the Staff's basic unity, its Group Spirit, its Staff Consciousness.

Every public institution, every business establishment, every school, club, hotel, factory, office building—in short, everywhere that people congregated in official Groups, there was a regular Staff on duty twenty-four hours a day.

They were Integrators. Glorified personnel men.

Electrodes were clamped on Kane's head and wrists. Something was strapped around his chest. Wires ran into a miniature Reacto. A stylus began to make jagged lines on a strip of moving tape.

"We're getting a complete personality checkup," the Staff said.

It was indeed complete. It was as complete as a personality checkup could be short of an actual dissection.

Kane looked at countless ink-blots. He was shown a great many pictures and whether he answered verbally or not was of no concern of the Staff.

Whatever his reactions were, they were all analyzed by the machines. Words weren't necessary. The Staff had a shortcut to personality checkups. From the mind right into the machine.

The Staff only interpreted the results, or maybe they didn't even do that. It was more likely that machines did that too.

Kane protested for a while, but he was too tired to protest very long. He asked them a great many questions, and they answered them willingly enough—up to a point. They were interested in his questions too. He was an interesting symptom, but actually he knew that they already had him pretty well tabbed.

They answered his questions the way big-hearted adults answered inquisitive children.

"We must," the Staff said, "determine why you don't fit in."

Kane talked about his work, his theories, his years of devotion to what he had always considered to be a contribution to society. They hardly seemed interested. What good was all that—astronomy and such—when a man was not happy with others?

"What about this aversion to people?" the Staff said, in a kindly way. "This—well—clinically, this de-grouping syndrome. This antagonism to the group spirit."

"You mean my reaction to Phil and his friends?"

"Your friends. Your Group," The Staff said.

"But I don't dislike those people," Kane insisted. "Certainly, I have no aversion to them! Hell, I don't even *know* them."

"But they're people," the Staff said. "Part of the family of man."

"I know that. But I was tired and wanted to sleep!"

"You'll find the true group Spirit," the Staff said. "Let us ask you this, Professor Kane. If you really had no aversion to people generally, why would you object to them being with you? Why should the presence of people disturb your sleep? Wouldn't a healthy person enjoy sleeping with others merely because they were there? Doesn't one sleep best among friends, knowing he isn't alone, knowing even his sleep is shared—"

There was a great deal more, but it all boiled down to the same thing.

Kane was wrong.

And he didn't have the right to be wrong.

They, or rather it, the Staff, seemed to concentrate on the whole question of why Kane had ever volunteered for a job demanding extreme isolation in the first place. The point was that apparently Kane had been anti-social, a Group Spirit deviant from the beginning.

Kane tried to explain it, calmly at first, then more emotionally. Either way, he knew that whatever he said was only additional grist to their syndrome recording mill. Being alone in order to do certain kinds of work demanding isolation seemed to be beside the point.

The point was that being on the Moon deprived a man of Groups. It was a kind of psychological suicide. Now that he was back home they would straighten him out. The question of returning to the Moon was ignored. To them, this was an absurdity. What did Kane want?

Kane was in no position to know what he really wanted—yet. They were going to help him decide what he really wanted. But they already knew that. It only remained for Kane to agree with them.

The majority was always right.

He explained his values to them. They listened. He told them that as far as he was concerned the social setup was now deadly, a kind of self-garrisoned mental concentration camp in which free thought was impossible. A stagnate, in fact a regressive state of affairs. Proficiency in skills would go, science would die. A herd state. Individuality lost. Depersonalized. Tyranny of the Majority. Integration mania. Collective thinking. Mass media. Lilliput against Leviathan....

But Kane wasn't happy, that was the important thing wasn't it?

Could a knowledge of how rapidly the Universe was expanding contribute to the happiness of a human being living on Madison Avenue in Manhattan?

Obviously the answer to that was no.

Kane was going to be happy. He wouldn't concern himself with the stars any more. He wouldn't practice a self-imposed barren isolation of himself any more. Kane was going to be happy. He was going to be one of the Group.

Time went by. He was given sedatives. He slept at last. He awoke and was tested and went to sleep again, many times. He was fed too, given injections with needles of energy and vitamins and proteins and glucose and carbohydrates, because he refused to eat any other way.

Vaguely he remembered episodes of babbling under the influence of hypnotic drugs.

He kept remembering the briefcase. In a dream the Group had it, throwing it around among them like a basketball. The clasp broke. The papers, thousands of papers spilled out and drifted away over New York and Kane was running through a maze looking up at them and then he was lost.

Now he knew what had happened to the other Moon ships, and to the rest of the Captain's crew, where they had gone to and never come back from.

Space was lonely and dark. Space was empty. Space was frightening.

They had gone back to the closeness and warmth and security of their Group.

How many were there left such as the Captain, and Kane—Kane for a while yet perhaps? How many were there?

Could he escape?

At some unrelated point on the Testing chart, the Staff closed up their briefcases, politely said good-bye, and left.

The data would be run through more machines.

Kane would be happy.

All he had to do was wait.

Kane awoke with a galvanic start and stared at the prison of his room.

The walls began coming alive. Phil, Laura, Lucille, Herby, Clarence, Jenny, Ben, the happy happy Group, always there, always waiting, always reliable, sharing everything, pleasure and pain.

"How we feeling now, Prof," Phil yelled. He was stark naked.

"You look so cuddly," Laura giggled, and for an instant there, Kane could almost feel her snuggling in beside him.

Kane lay there in a dim superimposed puzzle of furniture, moving forms, corners of rooms jutting out of the wrong walls, bodies walking through beds and one another, and then a naked figure curving into the air, falling toward him in a graceful arc, down, getting larger and larger, plunging right for Kane's face.

Kane rolled frantically. And then somewhere under him he heard a splash and there was the vague ripple of unreal water as Phil swam away across his cool blue pool.

There—that was Laura, only in a boudoir, standing before a mirror wearing only a pair of very brief panties, and nothing else. Her reflection in the mirror smiled at Kane as she brushed her hair.

"Morning, Prof honey. How we feeling this morning?"

It was morning. Some morning on some day during some year.

There was Lucille on this morning lying in a sunchair, her black hair shining in the sunlight somewhere. Probably in the Group house at Sunny Hill. In a while now, Kane knew, the Group would all go away together to their office, and they would do their work, concentrating on getting along together until they could return to Sunny Hill together.

Lucille was reading a newspaper, and she glanced up at Kane. There was a pale line around her mouth and she pulled her eyes quickly away as though she didn't want to look at him. She wasn't like the others. She was different. Of course. It had to be a matter of degree. Nothing was black and white. There had to be differences of opinion, some degree of individuality—somehow. Somewhere. Perhaps Lucille—

"Good morning, good morning to all of us!" Kane shouted suddenly.

"Did we have a good rest, Prof?"

Phil was yelling from his pool. He seemed greatly pleased with Kane's enthusiastic social response. Not that Kane was really trying to fool anybody. He was pretty sure the Staff wouldn't be fooled. Somewhere the machines were scanning the data. Soon, the Staff would have a full analysis of Kane, what was wrong, and what would make it right. What he should have done, and what he should be.

Jenny and Ben were making love on a couch. Kane tried to keep on watching them as though he suffered no embarrassment, but it was impossible.

"I've a full schedule planned for today," Phil yelled up. "Soon we'll all be going to the Office. You'll be going with us soon too, Prof!"

He would belong to the happy Group. Sharing everything. But maybe it wouldn't be this happy Group. Maybe the machines would decide that he belonged in some other Group. Whatever Group it was it would be happy. That was a fact.

Could he escape? Could he, perhaps, get back to the La Guardia Pits, and the Captain of the Moonship?

The windows still barred, paneled in metal. The door locked. If he managed to get out of this Single, say, and out of the Midtown Hotel, and into the street, then what?

That didn't matter. If he could only get that far—

Laura was standing there naked, close to Kane. "We're having our wedding at five," she whispered.

"Who?" Kane said, startled.

"Ben and Jenny. They're right for all of us together."

From a number of rooms, people were watching Ben and Jenny being right for all of us together, but Kane couldn't look.

"See us all," Laura shouted and dived through the floor. A spray of water spilled up and fell unfelt through Kane's flinching torso. Ben and Jenny ran away.

Kane was practically alone with Lucille. It was the first time in he had no idea now how long that he had been this much alone with any one other person.

She glanced rather sadly at Kane above the paper she was reading.

"You know how I feel, Lucie?"

She nodded, almost imperceptibly.

"How can you stand it, all the time this way?" he asked.

"Some of us learn to be in it, with a part of us out of it. A kind of self-hypnosis, a retreat of some kind. Into fantasy, that's what it really is. But—but I don't think any of us can keep on doing it forever. We will all give way completely—sooner or later."

"I've got to get out," Kane said. "Do you want to get out?"

"It's impossible to get out."

"I've got to try."

"What's the use of trying if you know you can't get away? Where can anyone go?"

"There must be people who break away," Kane said. "There have to be."

"There's supposed to be an underground, some secret group of some kind that helps people get out."

"Get out—where? Out of the country?"

"It's pretty much like this everywhere. But there are supposed to be areas where it isn't. Islands somewhere. Hidden places right here in the country. Supposed to be places in the Kentucky Mountains, and in New Mexico, places like that."

"The Moon," Kane said. "That's a place I know of. I've been there."

Her eyes were bright for a moment. "I know. It must have been wonderful. Why on Earth did you ever leave?"

"I didn't know what it was like here. And—my wife died. I wanted and needed another wife. More than a wife really. Someone who could share that kind of a life with me, someone who would be interested in the work too."

She turned quickly back to the paper.

"You might be able to get out of the hotel," she said. "But you would be too conspicuous."

"Because I would be traveling alone?"

"Yes."

"If you came with me, there would be two of us. We wouldn't be conspicuous that way."

He saw the flush move up through her face. "Is that the only reason?"

"You know it isn't."

She knew it. They both knew it and had probably known it for a long time. They had a lot in common, a minority of two.

And then he remembered. She wasn't really there in the Midtown with him. She was in Sunny Hill, wherever that was. They couldn't leave inconspicuously together because they weren't together now, and they couldn't get together without the Gang being together too.

The rooms, furniture, sounds, everything began to fade.

"Goodbye," Lucille said.

"Get sick or something," Kane said quickly. "Don't go with the Group to work. Stay there, wherever you are! *Stay there*—"

Faintly, her voice came to him out of a kind of melting mask of a face. "I'll try—"

Kane was alone in the single room and the door opened. The smiling Staff came in and shut the door.

The three of them stood there happily holding their briefcases.

"We're happy to report that we have completed your personality breakdown."

The word was a bit premature, Kane thought. "What is it?" he asked.

"Excellent," the Staff beamed. "You should never have been an astronomer. You took up that profession as a way of escaping from people. Actually, of course, you love people and hate your profession.

"Have you determined what I should be if not an astronomer?"

"Naturally, it's all in the breakdown."

"What is it?"

"Generally, you prefer physical work, not mental work. Mental work is a constant strain on your psychological balance. You have done it neurotically to reinforce your need to avoid people."

"Physical work? What kind?"

"Specifically, it seems that you are best suited for the profession of plumbing."

"Plumbing?" Kane said. "Plumbing what?"

"Plumbing, the art of pipe-fitting, the study of water mains, sewage lines, and so forth."

"Plumbing." Kane said.

"Of course, you react antagonistically to it now. But that will be changed."

Kane had nothing against plumbers or plumbing. Once, as a kid, he remembered having a long interesting talk with a plumber who was unstopping the kitchen sink. He had fascinating tools, and at that time, Kane had said he would be a plumber when he grew up. But he had also wanted to be any number of other things when he grew up, including an astronomer.

Now he had no desire whatsoever to be a plumber.

Kane drew the metal bedside table up hard and the edge of it caught number one of the Staff under the chin. Kane attacked, violently. He did it knowing that something more was at stake than his life—his identity.

Number one fell down on his knees and whimpered. He wasn't hit hard. But he squatted there blubbering as though he had suffered some horrible shock. Numbers two and three gaped as though equally shocked without ever having been hit at all.

That was Kane's initial advantage. The Staff seemed incapable of understanding that anyone would do what Kane was doing. Kane hit number two four times before number two covered up his face with his hands and started to cry. Kane ran him into the closet and locked the door.

Number three swung his briefcase at Kane's head, fluttering his other hand wildly. Kane was heavier than he should have been because he was accustomed to the Moon. But he was desperate and that was some compensation. He had some experience, a very little, as a boxer in college, but that had been years ago. But as little experience as he had at this sort of thing, he was way ahead of number three. Number three kept swinging his briefcase, and Kane hit him on the chin and then in the stomach and then on the back of the neck. Number three lay unconscious on the floor.

Kane stared at his bleeding knuckles a moment, then dragged Number one up onto his feet.

"You're going to help me," Kane said. "We're getting a saucer and then we're going to Sunny Hill. You know where Sunny Hill is?"

Number one ran his hand nervously through his dark brushcut. He had a boyish face that seemed deeply insulted by what Kane had done. Insulted and shocked as though he had been a good boy all his life and then someone had slapped his hand—for no reason at all.

Kane doubled his fists. Number one winced and looked shocked again, and very frightened. A great deal more frightened than anyone would be who was afraid only of physical injury.

"Yes, that's part of a big Group Housing Project downtown."

"Where can we get a saucer?"

"The roof."

"Unlock the door," Kane said. "And just pretend everything is happy and that we're relating beautifully to one another. Now listen—I'll kill you if you try anything else. I hope you believe it because I really will. What you fellows intend doing with me, as far as I'm concerned, is worse than murder."

They stepped onto one of several saucers decorating the roof of the Midtown Hotel. The rotary blades in the ten foot platform whirred under them, and Kane felt the saucer rise up to a thousand feet, then dip downtown. The air was full of them and only some kind of sixth-sense seemed to keep them from jamming into one another.

There was never less than two on a saucer. And Kane noticed that most of the saucers were flying in Groups like aimless geese.

Kane jumped from the saucer and ran across the roof landing of the Sunny Hill project building. There were a number of them like huge blocks arranged in some incomprehensible plan.

Kane glanced back to see number one leaping from the saucer and running in the opposite direction. Kane ran on toward the elevator. He knew he didn't have much time, but what bothered him was the authority he was running against. Public opinion was a general attitude, not a cop car, or a squad of officers with guns. Getting out of line, Kane figured, was usually its own punishment—isolation, loneliness, social ostracism.

But what about the exception? The guy who fought conformity and the majority opinion.

Who would they put on Kane? Or what? It would help to know what he was running from. What concrete force or power would try to stop him.

Then he saw her running toward him.

Her face was flushed and the wind blew her dress tightly against her slim body as she stopped and looked at him.

He took hold of her arm.

"We've got to hurry," she said. "The Group knows I've run away. The Staff will be after me."

Kane glanced at the elevator, then they ran back toward the saucer.

"You'll have to pilot this thing," Kane said. "It's a little crowded up there for me."

She started the motor and the saucer lifted abruptly. "The terminal at La Guardia?" she said.

"No. The ship's at least two miles from the Terminal. We'll go directly to the ship." He hesitated. "The only thing is—it isn't due to blast out of here until the 25th."

"That doesn't matter," she said.

"Why doesn't it? We're flaunting the law. They're after us. They won't let us just hide away on that ship until the 25th."

"They?"

He stared at her. "You said yourself we had to hurry, because the Staff—"

"But don't you see, there's no one to stop us now. The Staff at Sunny Hills could have, but here there isn't any Staff. There's none at the ship either, is there?"

"No."

"Well then, we'll just wait on the ship until—we go to the Moon."

"But you were afraid, Lucie. You talked about undergrounds, and how it was impossible—"

She touched his arm and then took hold of his hand. "You don't understand I guess. Maybe you never will."

"Understand what?"

"What it is to try to get away, be alone, be by yourself, when you can't. When no matter what you do you're with the Group, night and day, even in your dreams. You knew it for a while, but imagine it for years, not days. There's no place to hide. Wherever you go the Group goes with you. That's why I said you couldn't get away—"

"Then there isn't any law to prevent us from going to the Moon?"

"Only the law of the majority, of Public Opinion," she said. "But you can't stay here and fight it, not for very long. Finally you have to give in to it. You become what they are or go mad. And there are Groups even for them."

The saucer dropped down to the fog draped earth and they were walking toward the pits where the Moonship waited.

It looked like such a wonderful world, he thought. Everyone happy, everyone smiling all the time. No wars. No externalized authority.

The Manufacturers of consent. A quasi-totalitarian society in which means of communication had largely replaced force as the apparatus of compulsion.

Communication, fear, insecurity. In his isolation and insecurity, man clung to his Group, to the majority, the accepted opinions.

The majority did not need to force a man now. No need for police, or armies.

They *convinced* him.

The only way you could keep from being convinced was to get out.

The hatch slid open.

"Welcome aboard," the Captain said.

Milton Keynes UK
Ingram Content Group UK Ltd.
UKHW030403070224
437385UK00006B/366